FLIGHT SCHOOL

How to fly a plane step by step

Hello Flight School pilots. I wrote this book so you can learn how to fly a plane just like me. I'm a stunt pilot and I spend a lot of my time upside down. See you up in the sky! Nic

My father loved to fly, and inspired me and many others, so this book is for him.

Acknowledgments
Thanks to Max, Emily and Camilla, for your energy, guidance ... and indulgence; to Matt, Lucy, Russ, Willy, Pod, Jim, Jez and Dave, for your help with photos and contacts; and to Jeremy at AFE, for having supplied all the useful things pilots need. Thanks also to Katie-Sai, who read the book carefully, and can now fly!

On the cover
Front: top, Mikoyan MiG-29 (Mint Photography/Alamy); center, Stearman Model 75 (Skyscan/Corbis); below, mountains (blickwinkel/Alamy); back: top, Pitts Special (Woodbridge Aviation Images/Alamy); right, windsock (Angelika Stern/iStockphoto). Illustrations by Damien Weighill.

First published in 2012 in paperback in the United States of America by Thames & Hudson Inc., 500 Fifth Avenue, New York, New York 10110

thamesandhudsonusa.com

Library of Congress Catalog Card Number 2011937498

ISBN 978-0-500-65022-6

Printed and bound in China by Imago

Created by picnic
Editorial Deborah Kespert
Art Direction Belinda Webster
Design Katharina Rocksien

Illustrations
Black and white illustrations by Damien Weighill
Color illustrations by Katharina Rocksien

Photography
a = above, b = below, c = center, l = left, r = right, bgd = background

AgustaWestland: 6cr; Airbus S. A. S.: 2009 Computer rendering by Fixion–GWLNSD 7c, 2011 Photo H. Goussé: 43c, 2011 Photo P. Masclet: 30b, 42r; Alamy: David Askham 44l, Baum Images 33ar, blickwinkel 16–17b, 32–33b, 46–47b, front cover b, David R. Frazier Photolibrary, Inc. 43ar, Ernest Goodbody 34l, Andrzej Gorzkowski 33al, Thierry Grun–Aero 36l, Hornbil Images 6a bgd, 8–9b, 10–11a bgd, 12–13a bgd, 14–15a bgd, 18–19a bgd, 20–21b, 22–23a bgd, 26–27b bgd, 28–29a bgd, imagebroker 4b, 11cl, 20c, 31al, Interfoto, 37al, Riaan Janse van Rensburg 32ar, Dennis MacDonald 18br, Don Mammoser 26a, Chris Mattison 38l, Mint Photography 5cr, 11bc, front cover a, Anthony Nettle 14a, 27a, 35c, 41r, David Osborn 37c, Susan and Allan Parker 4al, 8ar, 9br, 35r, Frank Paul 35al, Charles Polidano/Touch The Skies 6b, Terry Smith 2, 16cl, Trinity Mirror/Mirrorpix 39, Colin Underhill 8cl, 23br, David Wall 34c, Woodbridge Aviation Images 37r, 3, 16ar, back cover a; Corbis: 27bc, Bettmann 7bl, 27bl, 45bl, Michael Cole 37cl, Daniel Hohlfeld/Sodapix 34r, Museum of Flight 36c, Skyscan 41cb, front cover c, Jim Sugar 32br, Josef P. Willems 14cb; Crown Copyright MOD 2011: Photo Sgt Pete Mobbs: 40r; DG Flugzeugbau GmbH: 6a; Dreamstime.com: Carmentianya 41ac, Ivan Cholakov 42l, 43l, Corepics Vof 13cr, imagecom 44c, Oleg Kozlov 40c, Kumikomurakamicæmpos 42c, Michael Miller 36r, Ken Pilon 25a, Trishz 28cl, John Wollwerth 45r; Eurofighter: © Aeronautica and Difesa 30a; Getty Images: 27br AFP, 35bl; istockphoto: dusko matic 4–5b, 6b bgd, 10–11b bgd, 14–15b bgd, 18–19b bgd, 22–23b bgd, 24–25b bgd, 28–29b bgd, Angelika Stern 5ar, back cover r; Nasa DFRC: 15c, Photo Tony Landis 45c, Photo Jim Ross 44r, Photo Carla Thomas 15a; Lucy Pope: 32l; Saab: Photo Stefan Kalm 41l; Shutterstock: valdezrl 30 bgd; Terrafugia: 45al; US Air Force: Senior Airman Julius Delos Reyes 7a, Staff Sgt Benjamin Wilson 40l, Virgin: Photo Mark Greenberg 4ar, 11cr, 43br

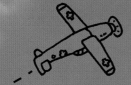

FLIGHT SCHOOL

How to fly a plane step by step

Nick Barnard

Thames & Hudson

Are you ready to sign up for Flight School?
Check out your timetable and prepare for take-off!

An-2

Are you ready to fly the world's biggest biplane?

Do you enjoy going to air shows and watching crazy stunts?

LY-AVI

OOL TIMETABLE

GROUND SCHOOL

AIRBORNE

Look out for these badges at the top of the page. They'll tell you whether you're studying in the classroom at ground school or mastering hands-on flight skills up in the air. Just like a professional pilot, you'll learn everything step by step.

Can you hear the roar of a fighter jet?

LEARNING TO FLY

Soaring up into the sky was just a dream for thousands of years. But today, here at Flight School, you can really become a pilot! What kind of flying machine would you like to take up into the skies?

DG-1000

AW119 Koala

Diamond Star DA40

⭐ GLIDER
For some pilots, their first experience is in a glider – a plane without an engine. Many advanced glider pilots compete in races for fun over long distances.

⭐ HELICOPTER
Have you ever taken a ride in a helicopter? If so, you'll know how flexible it is. A helicopter can take off and land in small spaces, fly straight up and down, and hover in the air, almost without moving.

⭐ TRAINER
All pilots at Flight School begin by learning the basics in a training plane. The cockpit is snug, with two sets of flight controls. The instructor sits next to you and guides you all the way.

⭐ FIGHTER JET

To fly in the military, you need to be highly experienced and trained especially for the job. If you're one of the best, you could fly a fighter jet like this one.

F-35 Lightning II

⭐ AIRLINER

Taking lots of passengers around the world, day and night, in all weathers, is a real challenge. Are you up for this job?

Airbus A330-300

Fit to fly?

You don't need perfect eyesight to fly a passenger plane – you can be a pilot even if you wear glasses. But if you want to fly a military jet, you do need perfect vision.

US pilot Chuck Yeager is a true flying hero who fought in World War II. Then, in October 1947, he became the first person to fly faster than the speed of sound in the rocket-powered X-1 plane.

FLYING KIT

LOGBOOK to keep a note of where you travel to and your flying hours.

VFR (VISUAL FLIGHT RULES) GUIDE to find airfields where you can land.

FLYING LICENSE which is up to date and signed by an instructor.

AERONAUTICAL CHART, also up to date, for route planning. A pilot must carry this at all times.

FIRST FLIGHT

Welcome to your first flight! Before you're old enough to get your license, you can still fly a plane with an instructor. You just need to be tall enough to reach the controls and see outside, with or without cushions!

PIPER CHEROKEE

G-BRBW

CESSNA 152

G-BWNB

G-BWNB

CHECKLIST!

KIT
Wear comfortable clothes, such as a t-shirt, jeans and sneakers. A leather flying jacket is for later.

SAFETY
Loose objects can roll around and jam the plane's controls, so always empty your pockets before you fly.

STRAP IN
Make sure you understand how the safety belts work.

Climb aboard
You'll be sitting in the captain's seat. This is usually on the left as you look forward. Don't worry if you feel confused – there's a lot to take in! All pilots feel like this at first.

Let the instructor plug in and put on your headset. Make sure it feels comfortable. Then adjust the microphone so that the instructor can hear you. When you hear the question, "How do you read me?" reply "Loud and clear."

PRIMARY FLIGHT INSTRUMENTS

There are four main instruments, called the primary flight instruments.
They help to answer important questions.

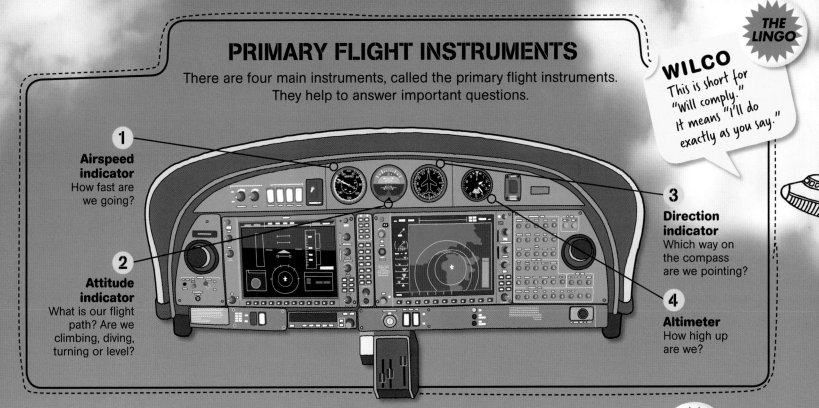

1 Airspeed indicator
How fast are we going?

2 Attitude indicator
What is our flight path? Are we climbing, diving, turning or level?

3 Direction indicator
Which way on the compass are we pointing?

4 Altimeter
How high up are we?

THE LINGO

WILCO
This is short for "Will comply." It means "I'll do exactly as you say."

How to ... get airborne

1. Start up

First, look out of the open window to make sure no one is in the way, then shout "clear prop." Turn on the ignition. Listen to the roar of the engine and the propellor starting up.

2. Taxi

Drive the plane along the taxiway to the runway. To steer, move the pedals beneath your feet in the direction you want to turn. To brake, press the top of the pedals.

3. Take off

Ready? In front of you, there's a lever called the throttle. Push it forwards. Then check the engine instruments and the airspeed indicator. Ease back on the stick. You're flying!

FAST FACTS

☞ On a sunny day, make sure you have a pair of sunglasses to wear.

☞ Be clear about who is flying the plane. When the instructor hands control over to you, he or she will say "you have control." You reply "I have control."

9

THE POWER OF AIR

Have you ever wondered how a plane stays up in the air? It's all to do with aerodynamics. This is the science of how air moves around an object such as a plane's wing. But before we explore aerodynamics further, let's get familiar with a plane's parts.

PARTS OF AN AIRPLANE

engine or engines
These provide thrust, or power. They are fitted to either the body of the plane or the wings.

fuselage
The pilot and passengers sit in the body. It is called the fuselage.

wings and tail
These are attached to the fuselage.

How does a plane fly?

Now it's time to concentrate. For an airplane to take off, its wings must lift upwards more than the airplane's weight pulls it downwards. It's that simple. When air rushes over a wing shape that is angled upwards to the flow of air, something amazing happens. The air is directed downwards and this creates an opposite force. The airplane moves upwards.

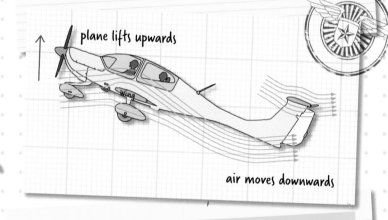

plane lifts upwards

wing

air moves downwards

What's drag?

Drag is the force that holds a plane back. As the plane pushes forwards through the air, the surface of the plane is resisted, or pulled backwards. When a plane flies level, which means it's not going up or down, lift and weight are in balance. The thrust, or power, balances the drag.

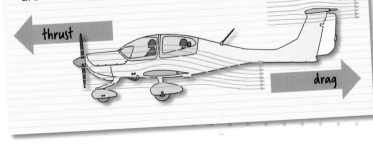

thrust

drag

How to ... see aerodynamics in action

1. Paper please

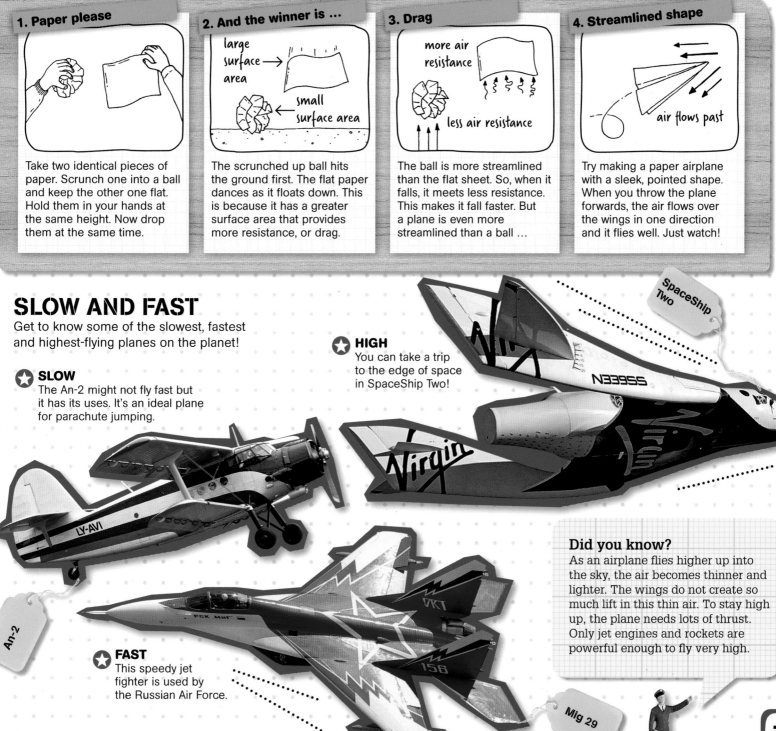

Take two identical pieces of paper. Scrunch one into a ball and keep the other one flat. Hold them in your hands at the same height. Now drop them at the same time.

2. And the winner is ...

large surface area

small surface area

The scrunched up ball hits the ground first. The flat paper dances as it floats down. This is because it has a greater surface area that provides more resistance, or drag.

3. Drag

more air resistance

less air resistance

The ball is more streamlined than the flat sheet. So, when it falls, it meets less resistance. This makes it fall faster. But a plane is even more streamlined than a ball ...

4. Streamlined shape

air flows past

Try making a paper airplane with a sleek, pointed shape. When you throw the plane forwards, the air flows over the wings in one direction and it flies well. Just watch!

SLOW AND FAST

Get to know some of the slowest, fastest and highest-flying planes on the planet!

⭐ SLOW
The An-2 might not fly fast but it has its uses. It's an ideal plane for parachute jumping.

⭐ HIGH
You can take a trip to the edge of space in SpaceShip Two!

SpaceShip Two

N339SS

Virgin

An-2

⭐ FAST
This speedy jet fighter is used by the Russian Air Force.

Mig 29

Did you know?
As an airplane flies higher up into the sky, the air becomes thinner and lighter. The wings do not create so much lift in this thin air. To stay high up, the plane needs lots of thrust. Only jet engines and rockets are powerful enough to fly very high.

11

TURNING

So you're off the ground and flying in a straight line but what do you do if you need to change direction? Take hold of the controls and learn how to turn your plane in the air.

HOW TO MAKE A RIGHT TURN

1 Start the turn
Start by moving the stick to the right. This will make the right aileron move up and the left aileron go down, creating more lift on one wing and more drag on the other.

FLIGHT CONTROLS

When you want to make a turn you need to move the ailerons on the wings. At the same time, you need to move the rudder.

ailerons
The ailerons are at the ends of the wings. Move the stick in front of you to control the ailerons.

rudder
The rudder is attached to the plane's tail and swings from side to side. You move it by pushing the pedals at your feet in the cockpit.

Turning tip
Always look all around you outside the cockpit before you turn. In particular, look where you are turning towards. You don't want anyone in your way! Got that?

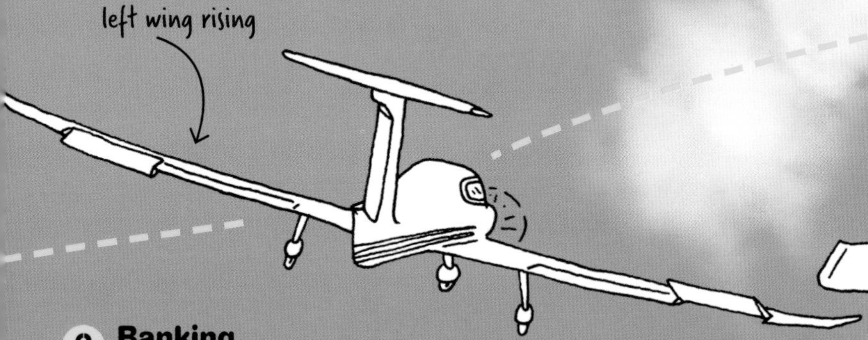

left wing rising

flying in a smooth turn

left wing still up

2 Banking

At the same time, push the rudder pedals with your feet to keep the plane balanced. Look out of the window and you'll see the left wing of the plane rising. You are now banking.

3 Stay in the turn

As you reach a steep-enough angle of bank, apply some more power and ease back a little on the stick to stop you from descending. Also move the stick to the center.

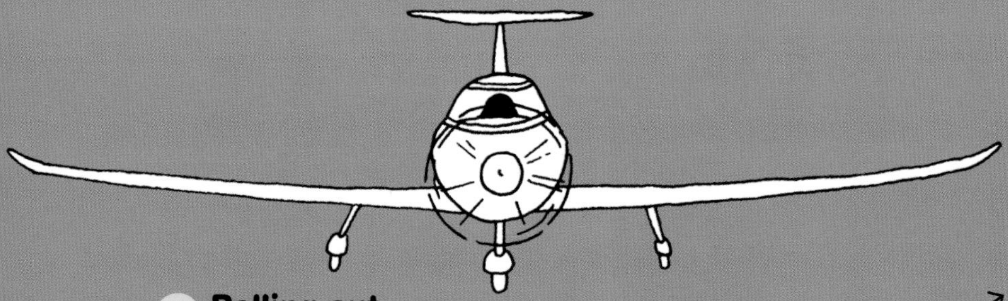

4 Rolling out

Now it's time to stop the turn. You don't want to go full circle! Ease the stick left, away from the turn. The wings will level off and you'll be flying straight ahead again but in a different direction. Good job!

Whether you are turning slowly or quickly, do it smoothly. Good pilots think about their passengers first. They fly carefully so that no one is frightened when the plane turns.

ENGINE POWER

Most planes have an engine to launch you into the sky and keep you up there. Your Flight School training plane has a gasoline or diesel engine inside the nose. There are also many other ways of powering an airplane.

⭐ JET ENGINE

A jet engine is much more powerful than a gas engine. It works best in planes that fly fast and high, so it's perfect for large passenger airliners and military jets.

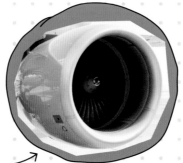

A big airliner needs lots of power to fly. All airliners have either two or four engines, which are fixed to the wings. A Boeing 747 Jumbo Jet has four engines.

Boeing 747-400

FAST FACTS

☞ The first jet-powered plane was the Heinkel He178, which first flew in 1939. It had a top speed of 375 miles per hour.

Helios

⭐ ELECTRIC POWER

In the past, electric motors and batteries were too heavy to power a plane. But today these motors can run on energy from the sun. Solar-powered Helios has flown higher than any other plane without rockets.

⭐ ROCKET MOTOR

To go super-fast, choose a rocket motor. The fastest-ever airplane, the X-15, was rocket-powered. It reached a speed of 4,520 miles per hour, about six times faster than the speed of sound!

X-15

What is thrust?

For a plane to move forwards in the sky, it needs thrust. A plane with an engine flies forwards because air is pushed in the opposite direction to the way it's flying. In a light aircraft, this happens when the engine turns the propellor. A rocket plane creates thrust by shooting out gases from its engine. Got that?

thrust moves plane forwards

air rushes past

How to ... see thrust in action

1. Blow up a balloon

Try this yourself. Find a balloon and blow it up. Hold it at the bottom between your fingers so the air can't escape. Lift it up high.

2. Let it go

Now let the balloon go. It'll zoom around crazily until all the air has escaped. The air rushing out of the balloon is pushing it forwards. That's thrust in action!

DIVE AND ZOOM

Pitts Special

Are you ready for your first stunt? A power dive! It's a thrilling feeling as you hurtle through the sky headfirst. Powerful jet fighters with really noisy engines have lots of thrust so they can zoom almost straight up after take-off. Hold on!

THE LINGO

A-FIRM
This is how pilots say "yes." It's short for "affirmative."

F-16

CHECKLIST!

When you dive you've got a lot to think about.

✔ Keep a lookout for other planes.

✔ Prepare to arrive at the right height and level off.

✔ Don't go over the safety speeds.

✔ Take care of your engine.

Air show action
If you want to see spectacular flying, check out a big air show. Up to 100,000 people may attend. There will be stunt planes like the Pitts Special as well as noisy jets like the F-16 and Eurofighter. Don't forget to bring your camera and earplugs.

POWER DIVE

Make sure you look at your flight instruments to check your progress as you dive.

1 Airspeed indicator
You'll be flying at high speed, but make sure you don't go over the top speed for the airplane.

2 Attitude indicator
This will show that the nose of the plane is down below the horizon.

3 Altimeter
The long needle will be moving quickly, to show your height decreasing at a fast rate.

4 Direction indicator
This should be in one single steady position except when you are turning.

How to ... look after your engine

FAST FACTS

1. Check temperature

slow airflow

When you climb steeply, you're flying slowly so there's less air flowing over the engine to keep it cool. You may need to lower the nose, which will increase your speed and the airflow to cool the engine down.

2. Avoid shock cooling

fast airflow

When you glide downwards, your engine isn't working hard and there is lots of air flowing over it. The engine could cool too quickly and be damaged. Apply power from time to time to keep the engine warm.

3. Don't rush

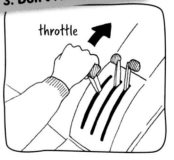

throttle

Your engine can be damaged! Treat it kindly and it will last longer. Always push forwards and pull back on the throttle smoothly and steadily while flying. Don't slam it open or closed unless it's an emergency!

☞ It's extremely noisy when you power dive. The engine is working furiously and you can hear the air rushing past too.

☞ In a fast dive, the controls are firm and hard to move. Get used to how they feel and work them smoothly.

☞ Most training planes climb at about 492 feet a minute. A modern stunt plane can climb at four times that rate.

PERFECT WEATHER

As a pilot, paying attention to the weather is really important. You don't need to be an expert but you do need to understand how the weather affects your flight. Always check the flying forecast for your route before you set off.

FACE THE WIND

In a training plane like yours, it's easiest and safest to take off and land into the wind. Make sure you're facing in the right direction!

WIND TIPS

☞ A headwind is a wind blowing against your plane from the front. It will make you fly slower and you'll use up more fuel.

☞ A tailwind blows in the same direction as you. This will make you go faster and shorten your journey time.

☞ Strong sidewind can push your plane sideways and off course. So regularly check your flight path.

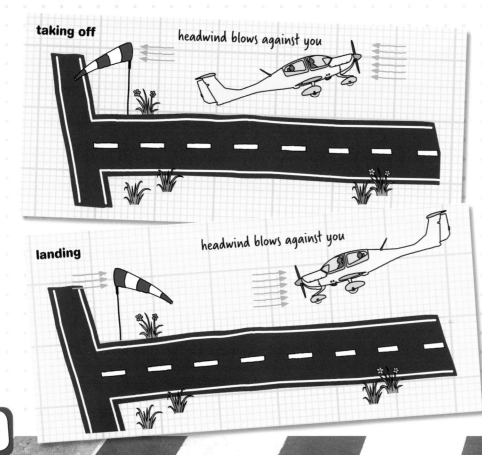

taking off

headwind blows against you

landing

headwind blows against you

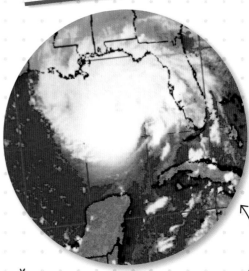

You can look up the weather forecast on your computer to find out what kind of weather is on the way. This picture shows a big storm, so there's no flying in this area today!

READ THE CLOUDS

All pilots should be able to recognize different types of clouds and the weather they may bring. Can you spot any of these clouds in the sky?

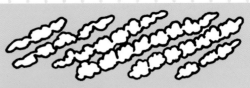

CIRROCUMULUS
Fluffy long ribbons. Usually seen in winter, they may mean a storm is on the way.

CIRRUS
Thin and wispy, high up. The weather may change.

CIRROSTRATUS
Hazy and almost see-through. There might be rain in the next 24 hours.

STRATOCUMULUS
Rows of fluffy balls. Usually a sign of dry weather.

STRATUS
A sheet across the sky often bringing drizzle and sometimes fine snow.

⚠ CUMULONIMBUS
Giant, tall clouds, gray at the bottom. A sign of extreme weather to come!

CUMULUS
Large balls of cotton wool. Fair weather but these clouds may only last for a few hours.

Weather quiz

Q: You've been flying your two-seater plane through cumulus clouds. There's a strong wind blowing and the clouds are getting taller. What should you do?

A: Steer clear of the towering clouds as there will be lots of turbulence and maybe lightning. You may need to land if the clouds join together and make a big thunderstorm.

FLYING SLOWLY

Most pilots love flying fast but if you really want to know your plane, then practice flying slowly. Watch out, though. Flying too slowly can make you stall, or lose lift. Are you ready to get out of that tricky situation right now?

CHECKLIST
Look out for these key signs that tell you you're heading for a stall.

✔ The plane starts to shake.

✔ The control stick shudders.

✔ The nose of the plane is up, but you're not climbing.

✔ You feel a loss of speed.

THE LINGO

ROGER
This is how a pilot says "message understood."

Stearman

Recover now
OK. You're fully stalled with no power. Your nose is dropping! When the instructor says, "Recover now," push the stick forwards. You'll enter a shallow dive. Ease out of the dive by pulling back on the stick, then apply power and off you go.

Did you know?
When your plane stalls, it doesn't mean your engine isn't working! But you will start to fall from the sky. All planes have a stall speed. This biplane stalls if it flies below about 50 miles per hour.

FLIGHT INSTRUMENTS

Take a look at your flight instruments. Can you work out what's happening?
Check out the answer at the side of the page.

1 Airspeed indicator
You're flying at low speed and it's gone very quiet in the cockpit. You start to feel some shaking.

2 Attitude indicator
Your nose is well above the brown horizon line. It's not where you want it!

3 Altimeter
Your nose is up but the altimeter is telling you that the plane is not climbing.

4 Direction indicator
You're not out of control and you're heading in a straight line but something is not quite right.

Answer: Watch out, you're about to stall!

How to ... slow down

1. Look around

First, look ahead and to the sides to make sure you have a clear path. When you start to slow down, the nose of your plane will go up and you won't be able to see in front of you.

2. Reduce speed

Now, reduce power by pulling back the throttle. Ease back on the stick too so that you stay at the same height. You'll soon realize how much less engine and wind noise there is.

3. Practice turning

Try a gentle turn. Can you feel how loose the controls are? Time to speed up. Increase power and ease forwards on the stick so you're back to cruising speed.

FLYING TIPS

☞ Make sure you know the stall speed of your plane when flying slowly. Don't fall below it.

☞ Practice flying slowly high in the sky so if you have a problem you can sort it out with height to spare!

FLYING RULES

Around the world, airplanes crisscross the skies day and night. To keep flying safe, pilots follow a set of international rules known as Aviation Law. Another set of rules governs when you can become a pilot. In the US, you can get your license as soon as you reach the age of 17.

FLYING DON'TS

Never head into a restricted airspace.

Never run out of fuel – you can't stop in the air.

NEVER CROSS THE PATH OF A PASSENGER JET.

NEVER FLY TOO LOW OR DIVE BOMB YOUR FRIENDS.

How to ... avoid other planes

1. Head to head

When two airplanes are approaching each other head on, both must turn right to avoid each other. They must do this whether flying through the air or moving on the ground.

2. Passing

In the air, pass to the right of the plane ahead. Keep well clear as the plane in front of you has right of way, which means it can go first if it changes direction across your path.

3. Give way

Powered airplanes must give way to airships, gliders and balloons. Airships give way to gliders and balloons, and gliders give way to balloons! Are you keeping track?

4. On the runway

When taxiing – that is moving along the ground – give way to any planes that are being towed. You must also give way to planes that are taking off or landing.

USING AN AERONAUTICAL CHART

When you fly, you need an up-to-date aeronautical chart, or flight map.
It looks pretty crazy at first but you'll soon discover it's full of important information.

Check it out
Pilots mark their flight route on the chart. Follow this route and check out all the things to look out for on the way.

Parachute drop zone
It's really important to give people who are parachuting their space.

Abandoned airfield
You may be able to land here in an emergency.

Heliport
This small landing space is for helicopters only.

Airfield
Training and light aircraft can land here.

Danger area
Stay away from a danger zone. It may be a military training area.

Bird sanctuary
Planes must avoid bird nesting and feeding areas.

Obstacle
Keep away from cell towers and telephone poles, especially if they have cables running between them.

Lit-up high obstacle
Very high things may have lights to help you see them at night.

G-BWNB

SAFE LANDING

No matter how much you love flying, you have to land sometime, and that takes skill and practice. Your goal is to come down steadily onto the runway, flying accurately and smoothly. Get ready for touch down.

One way system

The airspace around airports is really busy so all planes follow a one-way route whether they are arriving or leaving. This is called a visual circuit. When you practice taking off and landing, keep a lookout as you fly around the circuit.

CHECKLIST!

Make these final checks as you approach the runway. Say BUMPFF to help you remember!

✔ B – Brakes off
✔ U – Undercarriage (wheels) down
✔ M – Move engine mixture to rich
✔ P – Push propeller lever forward
✔ F – Check fuel on, both tanks
✔ F – Flaps down

VISUAL CIRCUIT

arriving

leaving at an angle

3 DOWNWIND

2 CROSSWIND

4 BASE   landing

taking off

leaving straight

5 FINAL   1 UPWIND

1 UPWIND
Take off into the wind. Climb at a safe speed.

2 CROSSWIND
In the air, make a left turn and fly across the wind. Level off.

3 DOWNWIND
Turn downwind and head straight. The wind will push you along. Make your checks.

4 BASE
Turn left when the end of the runway is behind your shoulder. Come down in height.

5 FINAL
Make a gentle turn and line up for landing. Check there are no other planes, then touch down.

Radio when you are ready to land. Once you've lowered your wheels, say "Final gear down and locked." When ground control replies "Clear to land, runway 24L," you can touch down.

This is a flap.

The wheels are part of the landing gear.

Airbus

How to ... land

1. Slowly please

The runway is in sight. Good! So the first thing is for you to ease back on the throttle to reduce power.

2. Lower flaps

Now start to lower your flaps. This will help you to fly safely at a lower speed. Do this in two or three stages.

3. Wheels down

Drop your wheels and lock them. On the final part of the approach, check again to be sure you have done this.

4. Touch down

When you cross the runway, pull back on the throttle to "Idle." Gently raise the plane's nose and touch down.

SOLO FLIGHT

Once you've shown your instructor that you can fly safely, the next step is to go solo – that means you can fly on your own. It's a scary but thrilling moment for all young pilots!

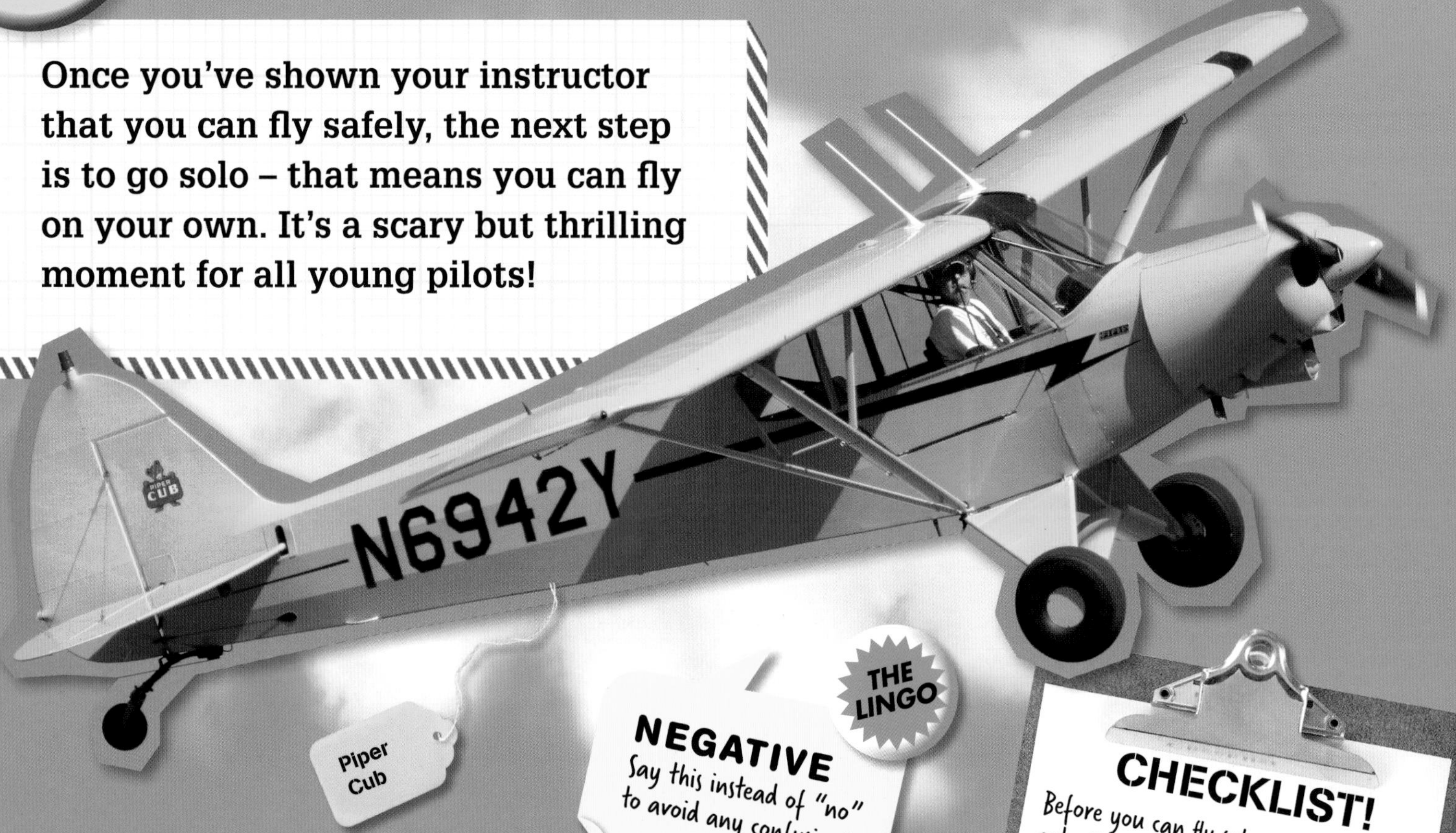

Piper Cub

N6942Y

THE LINGO

NEGATIVE
Say this instead of "no" to avoid any confusion!

Go it alone
You'll be in your training plane, so you should feel comfortable with all the controls. Try to relax even if you are nervous! Take off, then make one circuit around the airfield and land.

In time, as you become more confident, you'll be able to fly longer distances to far-off places in your favorite types of plane.

CHECKLIST!
Before you can fly solo, you'll need to get all these things under your belt.

✔ Learn and practice with your instructor.

✔ Show you can fly, take off and land.

✔ Pass a medical exam.

✔ Be 16 years of age. In a glider, you can be 14 years of age.

PILATUS
PC-21

HB-HZC

FAST FACTS

SOLO FLYING HEROES

There have been many daring solo flights in the history of flying.
Take a look at these famous pilots and their incredible achievements.

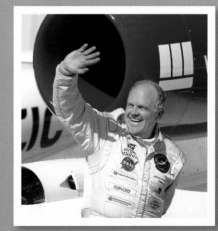

CHARLES LINDBERGH
The first pilot to fly non-stop across the Atlantic Ocean from New York to Paris in 1927. Lindbergh stayed awake during the 33-hour journey by eating sandwiches and slapping his face!

AMELIA EARHART
The first woman to fly solo across the Atlantic Ocean in 1932. Amelia Earhart then tried to fly across the Pacific Ocean in 1937, but she disappeared without a trace.

STEVE FOSSETT
The first person to fly non-stop around the world without refuelling in 2005. It took Fossett 67 hours and 1 minute to complete the challenge in his jet-powered Virgin Atlantic Global Flyer.

GOING PLACES

When you fly from one place to another, you've got a lot to do. You're flying the plane, talking on the radio and finding your way at the same time. Planning your route before you leave is really important so that you don't get lost.

How to ... stay on course

1. Think big

When you set off, always think about the whole picture. Look out of the window. Are you going in the right direction?

2. Be accurate

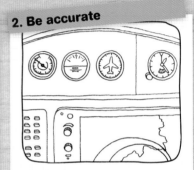

Fly accurately from the start of your journey. Check your dials to make sure you are traveling at the correct height and speed.

In the sky, take time to enjoy the amazing views from your cockpit. If you do ever get lost, remember small planes don't fly that fast, so you usually have enough time to correct your flight path.

MAYDAY
Say this three times in a row if you are in trouble. It will make all other pilots and air traffic controllers listen and help you.

THE LINGO

RADIO TIPS

☞ Even though talking and flying at the same time can be tricky, you must always think before you speak on the radio.

☞ Pause and listen carefully before you answer. Otherwise you might block out another message coming in.

☞ Be ready to take notes. The ground staff may ask you to repeat their instructions.

PLAN YOUR ROUTE

When you ride a bike, you follow a road or track, but in the sky there are no markings to help you, and you usually fly in a straight line. You can't stop and ask for directions either. So make sure you plan your journey carefully. Here are the tools you'll need.

FLIGHT COMPUTER
With the flight computer, you can work out how long the flight will take and how much fuel you'll need.

AIR CHART
Draw a straight line from the airfield where you're taking off to the one where you're landing. Make sure there are no areas you shouldn't be flying over.

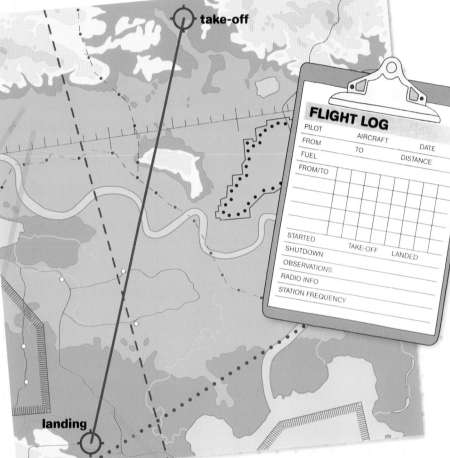

take-off

landing

MARKER PENS
Use permanent pens to mark the route on the chart so it won't wipe off.

FLIGHT LOG

FLIGHT LOG			
PILOT	AIRCRAFT		
FROM			DATE
	TO		
FUEL			DISTANCE
FROM/TO			
STARTED			
SHUTDOWN	TAKE-OFF	LANDED	
OBSERVATIONS			
RADIO INFO			
STATION FREQUENCY			

FLIGHT LOG
Fill in your flight log with all the details before you leave. Include where you're starting from and going to, the distance and flight times.

STOPWATCH
Start the stopwatch when you set off and check as you are flying along that you are on time at each reference point.

FLIGHT RULER
Measure the distance you will be traveling using your flight ruler and air chart.

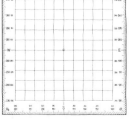

SQUARE PROTRACTOR
Work out the compass direction you will be flying along with your square protractor.

FLYING IN THE DARK

If you're a fighter pilot or captain of a Jumbo Jet, you'll have to fly at night and in bad weather. Sometimes you won't be able to see out of your plane at all! So here's a lesson on how to fly using only the instruments in the cockpit and runway lights.

Eurofighter

Landing in a storm

You're in a lightning storm but you've been cleared to land. Focus clearly on the instrument panel as you come down through the black cloud until the runway lights are in view.

KOREAN AIR

HL7611

A380

CHECKLIST!

Here are some rules for flying in the dark and through clouds, snow, rain, hail or fog.

✔ Plan your route carefully.

✔ Trust in your instruments even though it may seem scary.

✔ Always fly accurately and smoothly.

✔ Make small movements only with the controls. Don't panic!

Listen out for help on the radio. When you hear "Speedster 21, clear to land runway 24, caution extreme turbulence," you know you can go ahead but you're in for a bumpy ride!

This looks like the cockpit of a real plane but it's actually a flight simulator for an Airbus. Here pilots can pretend to fly in extreme conditions. You can get flight simulator games for the computer.

INSTRUMENT SCAN

When flying by instruments alone, you need to look from one to the other, changing your focus every two seconds. This is called the instrument scan. Always start with the attitude indicator as this is the most important dial. Practice scanning now!

airspeed indicator

attitude indicator

altimeter

turn co-ordinator

direction indicator

vertical speed indicator

FOLLOW THE LIGHTS

Most large airports have runway lights that change color as you approach them. The patterns help guide down the pilot.

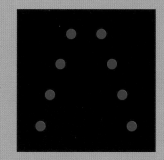

ALL RED
You're coming in too low. Climb immediately!

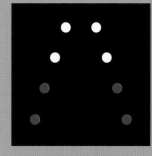

RED AND WHITE
This is spot on. You are safe to land.

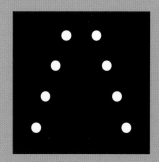

ALL WHITE
You're flying too high. Reduce your height to land safely.

Test yourself
Q: The runway is in sight and you can see the lights. They're red and white. Are you approaching at the right height?

A: Yes, you must be. Red and white lights mean you are on the right flight path for landing.

STUNT FLYING

For some pilots, flying stunts is the best thrill of all. You discover how far you can push yourself and your plane. If you practice hard enough, you could take part in a competition or thrill the crowd at an air show. So pick a plane and roll!

Tiger Moth

ZS-BGN

Sukhoi 29

HA-YAW

⭐ **OLD BIPLANES**
Flying stunts is known as aerobatics. Wartime pilots first developed aerobatic skills in biplanes to help them dodge, dive and zoom in deadly dogfights. You can still see biplanes like this one performing today.

⭐ **MODERN STUNT MACHINES**
Perhaps a modern stunt machine like the Sukhoi 29 is your thing? This plane is extremely powerful and can tumble and turn in a blur of speed.

Flying upside down a lot is really uncomfortable. Make sure you are strapped in tight or you will bang your head against the canopy.

⭐ COMPETITION FLYING

Aerobatics is a world championship sport, and there are competitions for beginners as well as experts. To win, you have to perform your stunts accurately and safely in a small space. Go for it!

⭐ AIR SHOW ACTION

You can't beat flying as part of a tight team at an air show. The crowds will cheer as you zoom through the sky, making different patterns, called formations, with the other planes.

Canadian Snowbirds

Extra 330SC

How to ... loop the loop

1. Power dive

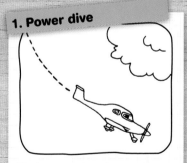

You've completed your checks so you're ready to go. Power dive at the top speed allowed for your plane. Watch the ground rush towards you.

2. Pull up

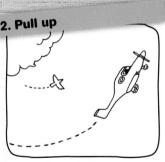

Now pull back on the stick and zoom up into the air almost straight. Keep on pulling firmly and steadily. It'll feel just like being on a roller coaster.

3. Upside down

When you're upside down, enjoy the feeling of floating and seeing the ground. Pull back less on the stick now to make the loop round in shape.

4. Level out

Ok, you're heading back down again. Can you feel yourself being pressed into your seat? Pull back on the stick again and level out. Fantastic work!

FAMOUS BIPLANES

Up until 1939, the start of World War II, most airplanes were biplanes. They had two main wings, looked magnificent and were nimble. But they were slow!

LONGEST WINGSPAN

BOEING STEARMAN

Built: USA
Wingspan: 32 feet
Top speed: 135 miles per hour
Range*: up to 500 miles
Number built: more than 9,700
First flight: 1934

⭐ The Stearman was a tough plane used to train US Air Force pilots in the 1930s and 40s. You still see them flying at air shows today. They are incredibly noisy!

SOPWITH CAMEL

Built: UK
Wingspan: 28 feet
Top speed: 115 miles per hour
Range: up to 300 miles
Number built: more than 5,400
First flight: 1916

⭐ This was the UK's most successful fighter plane during World War I. Its light controls and pair of machine guns turned it into a deadly weapon.

An-2

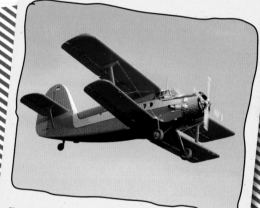

Built: Russia, Poland, China
Wingspan: 60 feet (upper wing)
Top speed: 160 miles per hour
Range: up to 525 miles
Number built: more than 18,000
First flight: 1947

⭐ Big, tough and powerful, the An-2 is perfect for parachute drops, carrying goods and crop-spraying. It can land on the roughest runways.

* Range means how far the plane can fly without needing to stop for fuel.

CURTISS JENNY

Built: USA
Wingspan: 44 feet
Top speed: 75 miles per hour
Range: up to 300 miles
Number built: more than 6,800
First flight: 1914

⭐ The Curtiss Jenny was built as a World War I training plane but it became more famous after the war as an incredible stunt machine that thrilled the crowds.

FOKKER TRIPLANE

Built: Germany
Wingspan: 24 feet
Top speed: 115 miles per hour
Range: up to 200 miles
Number built: 320
First flight: 1917

⭐ This highly aerobatic plane was flown by Germany's most famous World War I fighter pilot ever – Baron von Richthofen. He was known as the Red Baron.

DID YOU KNOW?
The first plane to fly was a biplane, made of wood, called the Wright Flyer 1. In 1903, it flew for 12 seconds at a speed of 6.2 miles per hour.

BUCKER JUNGMANN

Built: Germany and other countries
Wingspan: 24 feet
Top speed: 115 miles per hour
Range: up to 373 miles
Number built: more than 4,750
First flight: 1934

⭐ During World War II, the Bucker Jungmann was used to train German pilots. It was so fantastic at twisting and turning in the sky that it is still built today.

Biplanes usually had an open cockpit and no heating, so flying in one was often cold and breezy. To protect themselves, pilots wore goggles and a close-fitting helmet. A silk scarf and a thick leather flying jacket kept them warm.

WORLD WAR II FIGHTERS

During World War II, plane designers did their best to make planes fly faster, go further and carry more weapons. These are some of the most powerful propeller fighters ever made.

MESSERSCHMITT Bf109

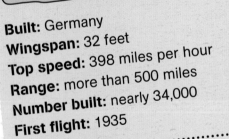

Built: Germany
Wingspan: 32 feet
Top speed: 398 miles per hour
Range: more than 500 miles
Number built: nearly 34,000
First flight: 1935

⭐ There were more of these fast little planes built than any other fighter in the world ever. They shot down over 15,000 other airplanes during World War II.

MITSUBISHI A6M ZERO

Built: Japan
Wingspan: 39 feet
Top speed: 331 miles per hour
Range: more than 1,740 miles
Number built: 10,939
First flight: 1939

⭐ The Mitsubishi A6M Zero was very light so it could turn better than other fighters. It had lots of guns and could fly a long way, but it was not strong or fast.

P-38 LIGHTNING

Built: USA
Wingspan: 52 feet
Top speed: 443 miles per hour
Range: up to 1,300 miles
Number built: 10,037
First flight: 1939

⭐ The P-38 Lightning looked really unusual. It was known as the "two planes, one pilot" by the Japanese, and was designed to fly at great heights.

MOST POWERFUL

World War II fighter pilots wore an oxygen mask while flying high up in thin air. They also carried a radio, a life jacket and a parachute for leaving the plane in an emergency.

YAKOVLEV YAK 3

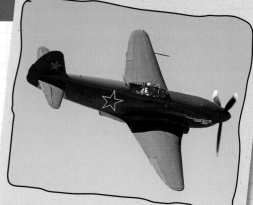

Built: Russia
Wingspan: 30 feet
Top speed: 407 miles per hour
Range: up to 405 miles
Number built: 4,848
First flight: 1941

⭐ This plane, loved by pilots, was small and light but also tough and extremely powerful. Many said it was a better fighter than even a Mustang or Spitfire!

P51 MUSTANG

Built: USA
Wingspan: 37 feet
Top speed: 437 miles per hour
Range: up to 1,650 miles
Number built: 16,766
First flight: 1940

⭐ The Mustang was such an incredible fighter that it was still flying for air forces in the 1980s. It was famous for protecting other bombers on long-distance missions.

HURRICANE

Built: UK
Wingspan: 40 feet
Top speed: 340 miles per hour
Range: up to 600 miles
Number built: 14,533
First flight: 1935

⭐ This tough UK fighter shot down more planes than the more famous Spitfire during the Battle of Britain. Later in the war it was used as a fighter-bomber.

DID YOU KNOW?
There are lots of World War II fighters still flying today. Look out for them at air shows during the summer months.

FLYING A SPITFIRE

This World War II Spitfire sounds terrific and flies like a dream! Imagine stepping into the cockpit and flying one yourself.

SUPERMARINE SPITFIRE

Built: UK
Wingspan: 37 feet
Top speed: 422 miles per hour
Range: up to 470 miles
Number built: 20,351
First flight: 1936

⭐ The Spitfire was built for speed, tight turns and fighting close to home. It was powered by a Rolls Royce Merlin engine and has become a flying legend.

flaps
Move this lever to lower the flaps when you're flying slowly or getting ready to land.

wheels
This sign tells you when your wheels are up or down. Don't forget to raise your wheels after take-off.

throttle
This lever is called the throttle. Push it forwards for more power. Be ready for the noise!

stick
Take hold of the stick and feel how easily the plane flies. Watch out for the brown gun-firing button!

dials

Here's the airspeed indicator and underneath it, the altimeter, so you can see how fast and high you're flying.

fuel

Keep an eye on your fuel levels here. You don't want to run out!

rudder pedals

Push the rudder pedals with your flying boots. Be ready to push left or right when you're turning.

FIGHTER JETS

Modern fighter jets are super-fast and powerful. Keep an eye open for them at air shows. But be ready to cover your ears and feel the ground shake as they zoom up sky high!

F-16 FIGHTING FALCON

Built: USA
Wingspan: 32 feet
Top speed: Mach 2+*
Range: more than 500 miles
Number built: more than 4,500
First flight: 1974

⭐ The design of this plane is over 35 years old but Fighting Falcons are still used by more than 25 air forces around the world. Pilots call it "The Viper."

SUKHOI 27

Built: Russia
Wingspan: 48 feet
Top speed: Mach 2+
Range: up to 800 miles
Number built: about 700
First flight: 1977

⭐ The Sukhoi 27 was one of the world's first super-maneuverable supersonic jet fighters. It can flip over, make tight turns and fly as slowly as a biplane!

EUROFIGHTER

Built: UK, Germany, Italy, Spain
Wingspan: 36 feet
Top speed: Mach 2
Range: up to 700 miles
Number built: about 275
First flight: 1994

⭐ This fighter was designed to do lots of jobs. It can shoot down planes, drop bombs and fire missiles at ground targets all on one mission.

* A Mach number tells you how fast a plane is flying compared to the speed of sound. If it's flying at Mach 2+, it's going more than twice the speed of sound.

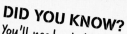

DID YOU KNOW?
You'll need a ladder to climb into a modern fighter jet – these planes are big! They're also strangely quiet once you're zooming along in the cockpit.

CHENGDU J-10

FASTEST

JAS 39 GRIPEN

829

Built: Sweden
Wingspan: 28 feet
Top speed: Mach 2
Range: more than 500 miles
Number built: more than 250
First flight: 1988

⭐ The Gripen is a tough, light fighter that can take off and land on short runways and even normal roads. This makes it really useful during wartime.

Built: China
Wingspan: 32 feet
Top speed: Mach 2+
Range: up to 675 miles
Number built: more than 190
First flight: 1998

⭐ The Chengdu J-10 was developed in secret. It has two extra small wings in front of the main wings to make it effective at twisting and turning in the air.

F-22 RAPTOR

Built: USA
Wingspan: 44 feet
Top speed: Mach 2+
Range: up to 500 miles
Number built: more than 165
First flight: 1997

⭐ Many people say the F-22 Raptor is the world's best jet fighter. It is a "stealth" plane, which means that it is extremely difficult for enemies to spot it using radar.

Jet fighter pilots wear a special suit, called a g-suit, and an oxygen mask to stop them from passing out while turning hard and traveling fast in their planes!

AIRLINERS

Big, fast modern airliners are always busy carrying millions of passengers and goods across the world. The next time you're at an airport, check out the different types.

BOEING 737

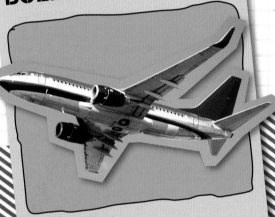

Built: USA
Wingspan: up to 117 feet
Top speed: 544 miles per hour
Range: up to 6,340 miles
Passengers: 215
First flight: 1967

⭐ The Boeing 737 is a medium distance plane. It is so popular that over 1,000 of these aircraft are flying right now and one lands and takes off every three seconds!

BOEING 747

Built: USA
Wingspan: up to 225 feet
Top speed: 614 miles per hour
Range: up to 9,200 miles
Passengers: 524
First flight: 1969

⭐ This plane is best known as the "Jumbo Jet." It is used to carry both passengers and goods. When loading goods, the whole nose of the plane opens up.

AIRBUS A320

Built: France, Germany, China
Wingspan: 112 m
Top speed: 537 miles per hour
Range: up to 7,500 miles
Passengers: 220
First flight: 1987

⭐ The Airbus A320 was the first airliner with a computer that could control some of the flying actions electronically. This is known as "flying by wire."

ATR72

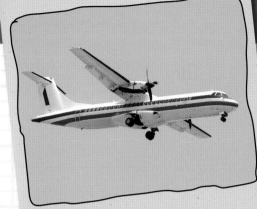

Built: France
Wingspan: 89 feet
Top speed: 326 miles per hour
Range: up to 823 miles
Passengers: 74
First flight: 1988

⭐ The ATR72 is a small airliner powered by turboprop engines. This type of engine is ideal for short-distance flights where speed is not so important.

DID YOU KNOW?
Many people think that the fastest airliner was the Concorde. Actually, it was a similar Russian plane, the Tu-144 known as Concordski. It travelled at 1,553 miles per hour!

LARGEST

AIRBUS A380

SINGAPORE AIRLINES

Built: France
Wingspan: 261 feet
Top speed: 634 miles per hour
Range: up to 9,500 miles
Passengers: 853
First flight: 2005

⭐ This plane is known as the "Superjumbo". It is so big that there is a camera on the tail to look forwards and help the pilot move around the taxiways.

VIRGIN GALACTIC SPACESHIP TWO

Built: USA
Wingspan: 27 feet
Top speed: 2,600 miles per hour
Range: to the edge of space
Passengers: 6
First flight: 2010 (a test)

⭐ This is the world's first spaceship for passengers! It is launched high in the sky from its mothership. A rocket engine fires it up into space.

CRAZY PLANES

Planes have always been made in different ways. Some were built to be small or light, others big, fast or cheap, and some planes have just been a bit crazy!

FLYING FLEA

Built: France and around the world
Wingspan: 20 feet
Top speed: 86 miles per hour
Range: up to 275 miles
Number built: unknown
First flight: 1933

⭐ If you want to build your own airplane, then this is the one to make. It's simple and it works. If you can drive a car, you can pilot a Flying Flea.

AIRSHIP

Built: UK, Germany, USA, China
Length: up to 250 feet
Top speed: 78 miles per hour
Range: not important, flies for days!
Number built: only a few
First flight: 1911

⭐ Airships are filled with a lighter-than-air gas called helium to keep them up in the sky. This airship has no metal frame inside and is known as a blimp.

SR-71 BLACKBIRD

Built: USA
Wingspan: 55 feet
Top speed: Mach 3+
Range: up to 3,350 miles
Number built: 32
First flight: 1964

⭐ Some experts say that the SR-71 Blackbird was the best spy plane ever. It flew incredibly high and fast, and was perfect for taking secret photos.

FLYING CAR

CRAZIEST

Built: around the world
Wingspan: different lengths
Top speed: up to 200 miles per hour
Range: up to 490 miles
Number built: unknown
First flight: 1937

⭐ For many years, people have tried to build flying cars and a few have taken off! The Terrafugia Transition, shown here, is the latest one being developed.

SUPER GUPPY

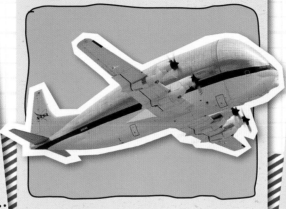

Built: USA
Wingspan: 153 feet
Top speed: 290 miles per hour
Range: up to 2,000 miles
Number built: 5
First flight: 1965

⭐ How do you carry parts of a space station or rocket into the sky? You use a Super Guppy! These planes were especially built to carry supersize loads.

DID YOU KNOW?
Flying all kinds of planes is really fun once you know how, but to be an expert pilot you still need to practice.

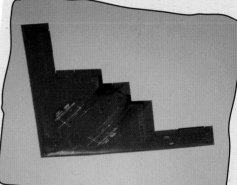

STEALTH BOMBER B-2

Built: USA
Wingspan: 172 feet
Top speed: Mach .95
Range: up to 6,897 miles
Number built: 21
First flight: 1989

⭐ Could it be a UFO? No, the B-2 is a top secret bomber that is almost invisible on a radar screen. It's also one of the most expensive planes ever built.

This pilot is Lincoln J. Beachy. He was known as the "man who owned the sky" and was probably the best ever stunt pilot in the early days of flying. He loved to loop the loop and fly upside down in a business suit!

FLYING TEST

SCORING
Give yourself one point for each correct answer. Then add up your points and check out your score.

Put yourself in the pilot seat one more time and take this sky-high flying test. You can find all the answers in the book if you get stuck!

1
You've completed all your checks and you're lined up on the runway. How should you increase power for take-off?

a) push the throttle forwards
b) pull back on the stick
c) blow really hard

2
When you fly, the engine thrusts you forwards. What opposite force holds you back?

a) an electromagnetic shield
b) a strong wind
c) drag

3
You're flying along and want to turn. What should you do before you change direction?

a) shout "mind out"
b) turn on the radar
c) look around the sky carefully

4
If you want to fly really high and extra-fast, what sort of engine is best?

a) electric
b) rocket
c) steam

5
You need to say "yes" while talking on the radio. What words do you use?

a) roger dodger
b) ok
c) A-firm

6
As you slow down, how do the flying controls feel?

a) loose and floppy
b) solid as a rock
c) out of control

7
You see a plane coming straight towards you in the sky. What do you do?

a) close your eyes and duck
b) climb above it
c) turn right

10

Oh no! There's a problem with the engine and you need help. What do you say on the radio?

a) help, help, help
b) mayday, mayday, mayday
c) golly, golly, golly

11

You're in cloud and flying by instruments. What instrument should you look at most?

a) the altimeter
b) the attitude indicator
c) the clock

12

You've passed your test and want to go flying. Which of these three things must you carry with you?

a) a bowl of cereal
b) a protractor
c) an aeronautical chart

9

Your instructor has sent you off flying on your own for the first time. What has he asked you to do?

a) take off and do some stunts
b) fly over your house
c) one circuit and land

How did you score?

0–5 Whoops! Get back in that training plane and start again.

6–9 Well done. You're on your way to going solo.

10–12 Top marks! What do you want to be – a fighter pilot or captain of a Jumbo Jet?

Answers
1a, 2c, 3c, 4b, 5c, 6a, 7c, 8a, 9c, 10b, 11b, 12c

8

You are on the final approach to land. What must you never forget to do?

a) lower the wheels
b) raise the flaps
c) wave to the people below

FLIGHT SCHOOL CERTIFICATE

CONGRATULATIONS!

You have now completed your training and been awarded your Flight School Private Pilot License. Happy landings!

Signed

Nick Barnard

Flight School Chief Pilot

47

INDEX

AIRCRAFT NAMES